Thank you for reading.

Please reach out to info@bluecordmgmt.com for bulk pricing and customization of copies of this book for your team and organization.

Receive daily sessions via text message at: https://lrn.st/lead

You can learn more about BCM's leadership training opportunities at
https://leadership.bluecordmgmt.com/training

Daily Leadership Reflections

Reflections

A Guided Journal
For New Leaders

Ed Brzychcy

Blue Cord Management, LLC
Boston, MA
www.bluecordmgmt.com

ISBN: 9781081336783

Dedication

This book is dedicated to all fallen service members who have made the ultimate sacrifice since 9/11.

They are the true heroes.

We are proud to donate a portion of all book sales to help support some of the many agencies who aid and assist returning, transitioning, and disabled veterans and military service members.

Acknowledgements

A very special thank you to everyone who has made this first book possible.

No great undertaking is ever accomplished alone.

This is especially true both when starting a business and writing a book.

* Thank you to the many NCOs and Officers I served with who gave me the inspiration to build my career both while I was in the service and after.

* Thanks to all my friends and family who have stood by me and believed in me through every crazy iteration of my ideas on what I want to do and what I want to build.

* Thanks to everyone who read a draft copy and provided all-important feedback

* And thanks to Megan Burns, for editing and translating what I wrote into something more comprehensive and understandable.

Introduction:
What to do when you're new.

Knowledge is a leader's most valuable asset. It's also a risky blind spot. What you know, or think you know, may be wrong, and it may not be enough for the challenges you'll face down the line.

A leader can never have enough knowledge.

New managers and supervisors as well as experienced organizers face constant leadership challenges in their roles, creating the need for new ideas to add to their experience and reinforce best practices. New leaders face a critical challenge as they start their new roles. For many new leaders, their first 30 days can often be the most critical and can set the tone for their entire careers.

If they fall short, then it is not only these aspiring leaders who can harm their careers, but also the careers of their team members, and the success of their projects.

We are aiming to help ensure our readers' success by providing some thought-provoking, insightful questions to identify crucial knowledge gaps and help new leaders start on the right foot when entering their roles.

This book is a 30-day guide designed to help take stock of current knowledge, question assumptions, find gaps, and begin to fill them. It is intended to push leaders out of their comfort zones towards creating new leadership skills, habits, and acumen.

Table of Contents

Day 1 – Welcome to Leadership

Welcome to your first day as a leader. Congratulations on your new role, and the new responsibilities that come with it.

Leadership is the ability to create a vision more significant than yourself and inspire others to help you achieve it. It's the ability to rally a team to accomplish something one person can't do alone. That's not easy. It requires a wide range of skills including communication, the ability to understand and empathize with everyone around you, and the capacity to think strategically and find smart solutions to complex problems.

Leadership can be a thankless role. When you do it well, you can be nearly invisible. Your job is to stand by and make sure things are managed appropriately without getting in your team's way. However, when things are going wrong or are changing, it's your job as leader to step to the front, guide your team, and facilitate a successful outcome.

We all have leadership role models, people we look up to and aspire to emulate. Reflect on who helped make your leadership position possible.

A Role model for me is:

My boss at my first job, Jim.

They influenced me by:

Consistently showing how much they cared, especially when I messed up.

Together, we accomplished:
We did this by:

Over-Achieving our team's goals
Working hard, making sure that our work is timely and correct, and by his taking the time to make sure I know everything that I needed to become successful.

Day 2 – The 5 Components of Leadership

Building all the skills needed to be a great leader can feel overwhelming, so let's break it down a little. Influential leadership has five components:

1. Be visionary

2. Set the example

3. Build frameworks

4. Learn and grow continuously

5. Be able to make a decision

We'll explore each of these topics in the next few days, but for now just think about your overall goals.

What do you want to accomplish in the next 30 days?

Three things that I want to learn in the next 30 days are:

1. I want to get to know my team better.

2. I want to become more comfortable in my role as a leader.

3. I want to become a better communicator.

Day 3 – Developing Your Vision

Vision sets great leaders apart.

Think of the tasks your team needs to accomplish as a mountain. Do you have a clear sense of how you're going to get to the top?

A leader's vision is what gives their team purpose and direction. It is, by definition, more significant than the leader alone. It has to be bold enough to keep you (and them) awake at night, and exciting enough to get everyone up in the morning ready to start the day.

Your vision must be rooted in your company's overall vision, but be specific enough to explain how your part of the organization contributes to that overall mission. I call this a **relative vision**.

Reflect on your team's role in the broader organization:

My organization's mission is:

This goes beyond the poster on the break room wall. Why do we do what we do?

My part of this is:

What is your team's role? What do you contribute as a group to the larger organization?

My team contributes by:

What does your team do? Why do you do it? If it is only for a paycheck you're reading the wrong book.

Day 4 - Setting the Example

It takes a team to accomplish anything significant, and as a leader, it's up to you to be the role model they need. "Do as I say, not as I do" won't cut it. Great leaders are less talk, more action.

Attitude is everything when it comes to setting a good example. You must maintain a can-do attitude, put your best face forward, and be the ultimate champion for your vision. You must be willing to take less credit when your team is successful and more responsibility when they fall short.

Emotion and behavior are contagious, and because you're a leader, what you do can have a much more significant impact and spread faster. That's what influence is all about.

Reflect on what kind of attitude you want to project to the people around you.

The attitude that I wish to project is:
I want to constantly remain positive and project a "can-do" attitude.

I can do this by:
Remaining optimistic in the face of adversity.

The challenges are:
Not allowing setbacks to set me back, constantly moving forward despite it looking like we're not making progress.

Day 5 – Build Frameworks

Does your plan include the part where it doesn't work?

Leaders need frameworks because no plan survives first contact with reality. There will always be something forcing you to re-think and adapt. You have to keep this in mind when building your plans and projections. Circumstances, situations, and people are all dynamic, but the right frameworks help you and your team adapt and learn as you go. They provide contingency plans so you are never blindsided or caught off guard.

The core of your framework is the fundamental skills you and your team need to be successful, the ones that help you solve whatever problem may arise. Everything you do should be aimed at maintaining this strong set of fundamentals so you don't have to reinvent the wheel when things change.

Reflect on the framework of skills and practices your team needs:

Some of the fundamental skills for my team to accomplish their mission are:

Taking calls, making outbound sales, appropriately filing reports, performing a strong analysis ...

I can better integrate building these skills into my teams daily practices by:

Keeping closer track of my team's progress on tasks.

My team members can improve their skills by:

Providing robust feedback among one another.

Day 6 - Learning Continuously

We learn from everything that we do.

Great leaders are intimately aware of their surroundings and always mindful of what improvements can and should be made. They take suggestions from everyone, keenly aware that they don't – can't – know everything.

Great leaders seek knowledge from those who are more informed on a topic that they are or people with a different perspective than their own. They learn from their mistakes and bad experiences. They cultivate the attitude that mistakes aren't failures; they're stepping stones to learn and grow.

Failure only happens when a leader stops moving forward. True leaders never quit. They know nothing is ever useless; it can always be positioned as a lesson in what doesn't work.

Real failure happens only when you give up. Everything else is a learning experience.

Reflect on a mistake that you made and what you've learned from it.

I made a mistake by:

Showing up late 5 days in a row simply because I was unmotivated to go to work.

From this mistake I learned to:

Keep better track of my attitude, and try not to let my personal life interfere with my professional life.

I have put ____ in place so that I do not make this mistake again.

Better self-care regimens, and making sure that I have a place to vent when I need to.

Day 7 – Decision Making

We often put pressure on ourselves to make the perfect decision. The weight makes it easy to overthink your options and get stuck in analysis paralysis. As a leader, you can't afford that.

Not making a decision is often worse than making the wrong decision.

Hesitation, bias, and fear can hinder even the most experienced leaders. They're all part of being human. To move forward and grow, leaders know they have to have new experiences and hesitating gets in the way of that.

It's important to note, though, there's a difference between pausing and hesitating. When you're delaying a decision, ask yourself: What additional information am I looking for, and how can I get it? Nine times out of ten, you can find the missing information faster by trying something than waiting.

Leaders also have to be clear about the decisions they're making, or not making. Team members are continually looking to you for guidance. If you're pausing, tell them why. If you're acting, tell them what signs and signals you want them to look for as events unfold.

Reflect on a decision which you are currently struggling with.

I need to decide:

What is an upcoming conflict that you want to make a decision on?

3 things that I need to know before I make this decision are:

What is the situation? What are the variables? How will people react to your decision?

I can get this information through:

What are some open-ended questions to ask about your above answers?

Checkpoint 1:
Check your Vision

Having a robust relative vision is of utmost importance in leadership at every level

It is worth spending some more time to refine your relative vision for your team.

1. Recap your relative vision for your team here:

_____

_____

_____

2. Next, test your vision to make sure that it is impactful.

One way to do this is to use the "Common sense—Not" test. Go back, and look at your vision, and look think, "What if we decided *NOT* to do this?"

If not doing it seems ridiculous the vision is not unique, differential, or advantageous. Start to think bigger, bolder, and with some more clarity towards your ideas.

For example if your vision is: "We will provide the greatest customer service." it can be looked as "We will NOT provide the greatest customer service.", which makes no sense. Of course, we're going to provide excellent customer service.

Does your vision pass this test? If not, clarify and refine further below.

_____

_____

_____

Day 8 – Keys to Communication

Leadership is never a solo activity. It requires us to talk to other people, and often have deep and difficult conversations. How you handle those communications shapes your influence and credibility as a leader.

There are natural barriers to excellent communication. There's no guarantee that what you say is what other people will hear. Still, you must seek to ensure that your message is clear and actionable.

One way to do that is to pay careful attention to non-verbal cues and body language such as the way people are sitting or standing, their posture, and signals of interest and understanding.

In verbal communications, strive to be clear and coherent. Choose your words carefully, making sure you don't lose the audience to jargon or words that are overloaded with too much ambiguous meaning.

One crucial step in communication that is often missed is asking for clarification to make sure that your message was received, understood, and will be acted on appropriately.

Think for a moment about a time when someone has misunderstood you, or you have misunderstood someone else.

A misunderstanding in my communications was:

I recently submitted a report where some of the information was misinterpreted.

A positive change - such as word choice, clarifying questions, or non-verbal acknowledgment - that could have prevented this is:

We overlooked how two different areas were related, and missed the deeper relationship between them.

I will prevent this from happening the next time that this issue comes up by:

Better understanding of the factors that I'm reporting on. Asking better questions to get to understand the situation at a higher level.

Day 9 – The Importance of Listening

We were born with two ears and one mouth and should strive to use them in that ratio.

To guide your team toward success, you have to know what their needs are, what changes they see, and what lessons they're learning, and how they can help the overall mission.

Leaders have to be able to ask the tough questions of anyone and everyone – our teams, peers, mentors, and even bosses. Then we have to listen to their answers.

Listening involves taking the time to reflect on, assess, and respond appropriately to someone's statements or questions in a way that's open-minded and non-judgmental.

Be ready to admit when you don't understand something you hear, to voice disagreement with someone's viewpoint, or to provide constructive criticism. We do all these things to help people grow.

Reflect for a moment on a conflict you're having or have had.

What assumptions am I making about the situation?

There is a conflict simmering with an adjacent team leader and their interactions with my team members.

Some clarifying questions to help my understanding are:

Why are they approaching me team members this way, are our lines of responsibility clearly drawn?

I can frame this conversation in a positive and constructive way by:

Asking why they are doing what they're doing in that manner, making sure that they are going through me to have certain conversations with my team members.

Day 10 – Build Self-Knowledge

It can be hard to assess yourself, but self-knowledge is critical to great leadership. Some key questions you should be able to answer are:

- What are my strengths?
- Where can I improve?
- Can I find others who are good at things I'm not?
- How can I take care of myself and manage my stress?

The most considerable challenge here is accuracy. We each have our own implicit biases, including the tendency to see ourselves in a positive light. To grow and improve, we have to be brutally honest.

From there, you can build on your strengths by honing adjacent skills that magnify your abilities. At the same time, you can mitigate gaps in your knowledge and skills by delegating tasks or building the necessary support systems.

Ask three people, a mentor, peer, and co-worker, what they feel your greatest strengths are and where *they* think you could improve most.

My Strengths are:

Communicating, Building Relationships, Training my team, Technical Expertise

Areas I can improve are:

Learning the updated computer system, Handling Conflict, Asking better questions

I can make these improvements by:

Finding a mentor, attending a class, finding a new relevant podcast

Day 11 – Creating an Internal Knowledge Base

Leaders need to know what's going on within their teams and roles, and what's changing.

That knowledge can't be high level. We have to know our team members, higher-ups, peers, and business environment in detail. We also have to know what tasks we and our teams are responsible for, the standards we have to meet, and the tools or equipment we use in daily work.

As a leader it's your responsibility to stay ahead of any and all changes in these areas. Great leaders also anticipate blind spots—things they don't know or might not see coming.

Thankfully, you're not starting from scratch. It helps to take an inventory of your existing knowledge and use that to help you keep up.

Reflect on what you know about you team.

My team members are:
A few facts about my team members are:

List your team members and their roles.

What don't I know about my team members?

Go beyond simple skills, who are they as a person, what are their likes
and dislikes, what are their aspirations?

**The tools and techniques that my team uses to accomplish their job
are:**

What are some of the tools, systems, procedures, and standards that
your team has?

Day 12 – Seeing the Big Picture

You may know everything there is to know about your team but to be a great leader; you also have to see the bigger picture.

No one has a crystal ball – we can't tell what our organizations will look like in the future. However, you can learn as much as possible about the disruptions, changes, and influences acting on your activities now.

Leaders know which outside forces affect their teams most and can guide people to adapt as needed.

They refuse to accept "We have always done it that way" as a rationale because it's their job to prepare their teams for the future, even when that means moving outside everyone's comfort zone.

Reflect on some things that are changing in your market and industry.

Some potential changes in my market and industry in the next 3-5 years are:

Technological developments, changing customer preferences, changing suppliers, workforce demographic shifts

They will affect me an my team by:

How will these relationships change? What impact will outside changes have on your team?

A good source to find new information about these changes and ideas is:

Trade magazine and conference, podcasts, news shows, mentors in adjacent divisions and industries

Checkpoint 2:
Know Your Surroundings

We have many different facets and variables in our roles to fully understand and act upon as leaders. We have talked about the three tiers to building our knowledge, ourselves, what's happening immediacy around us, and what outside forces affect us, our team, and our mission.

Understanding all of these areas requires impartial and in-depth communications to get to the root of what is happening in each area. Let's continue some of the work from the last few days.

Look back at Days 10, 11, and 12.

What is your primary driving force in your leadership role. Be honest, and write down why you want to be a leader.

_____

_____

_____

Given your team's mission and goals, how can your motivation help them reach these?

_____

_____

_____

What's happening around your team? What can you begin doing to get ahead of any changes and disruptions that are coming your way?

_____

_____

_____

Now take each of these areas and ask your team what they think.

Day 13 – Effective Delegation—Part 1

It's a simple fact; we can't do everything ourselves. In fact, as leaders, we should not be solving our people's problems – we should be teaching them how to figure out the solution on their own.

Delegating allows us to do that. It's not just a way to get things done; it's a learning tool. Giving people tasks they don't ordinarily do provides enrichment, personal and professional growth, and can lead to an expansion of job responsibilities.

Everyone learns slightly differently; however, we have no opportunity to learn and grow if we're not experiencing new things. As the leader of your team, it is your responsibly to see that your team is consistently pushing out of their comfort zones and embracing new ideas, change, and incremental improvements in their daily activities.

Many leaders are uncomfortable delegating because they're unclear about three things:

1. The tasks they want to delegate
2. The team's ability to complete those tasks
3. How to evaluate the work to make sure it's successful

That last one is particularly important. When you delegate, you're sharing responsibility, not passing the buck. The buck still stops with you. You are ultimately responsible for making sure the work gets done well. However, through proper delegation you can do that and stretch your team at the same time.

Take an honest look at one task that you want to delegate out.

I want to assign task _____ to _____.

One task that you want to see a team member embrace, own, and start performing.

What skills, techniques, and equipment will this person need to accomplish this task?
Do they have all of these?

What are the components of this task? Think of skills, equipment and other tools, what procedures and standards are in place for performing this task?

How will I know if they completed the task successfully?

What training and preparation needs to be put in place to accomplish this task? What helps you perform it?

Day 14 – Effective Delegation—Part 2

Yesterday, you thought about what you'd like to delegate. Today, reflect on how reasonable it is to delegate that work to the person you had in mind.

Delegation can build trust between you and your team only if the tasks you delegate are good fit for them, meaning they are:

- Within their realm of expertise
- Manageable in the time constraints
- Realistic in its outcomes

If those three things aren't true, you must find a way to make them true. Transfer or teach the expertise they're missing, ensure people members have adequate time (e.g. by taking something else off their plate), and clearly articulate what success looks like.

You also need to follow up in a reasonable way. Great leaders check in regularly on the status of the work they've delegated; they DON'T hover over every detail. You have to work with your team to establish specific, reasonable checkpoints based on experience and expectations.

Reflect on the task you wrote about yesterday.

Is the person truly ready to accomplish this task?

Looking at yesterday, is everything in place? What gaps still exist in their knowledge or other readiness in accomplishing this task?

Will they learn and grow from the experience of doing it?

What metrics are used to measure success? What are some future steps for your team member?

What schedule do I propose for following up?

Are there appropriate times and benchmarks to measure progress?

Day 15 – Self-Awareness and Regulation

Before you can lead others, you have to lead yourself.

Great leaders have high emotional intelligence. One piece of that is self-awareness or self-knowledge, which you thought about back on Day 10. Good self-awareness gives you the confidence to handle new and different situations.

Knowing yourself isn't enough, however. The other side of emotional intelligence is self-regulation – being able to manage your own emotions so you can do the right thing for the team in any situation.

Self-regulation is particularly important when things change, don't go well, or we're dealing with something new. It helps us maintain that can-do attitude even the face of frustration, setbacks, and disappointment.

Think back to your conversations from Days 10 and 11.

Thank about a time when you've managed your own emotions well.

When have you have a hard time keeping your cool?

Think about how you act under pressure. Do you shut down, get angry, or have other ways of experiencing stress?

How can you begin to build on your strengths and apply them to other situations?

Day 16 – Building Motivation

Our team's inspiration and motivation is a direct reflection of our own.

Teams will mirror their leaders, especially when it comes to your overall level of motivation. If the boss doesn't care, why should they?

The specifics of what motivates people are different, though. You have to ask team members what their goals are, where they see themselves and the team in the future, and what success looks and feels like to them. Just as you have a relative vision for the team, people have relative visions for themselves.

Be prepared – this can lead to some awkward and difficult conversations. The truth about what your team wants may not match your preconceptions, and you can't change their values or goals. Leaders have to adapt, learning to express appreciation, and describe team members' contributions in a way that feels satisfying to *them*.

Getting to know what motivates your team builds a bond that enables you to rally them. When you as a leader are working to help your people meet their career, professional, and personal goals, they feel valued and supported, which in turn makes them work harder to achieve team goals.

Think about the members of your team.

What are their goals in 90 days, 1 year, and 5 years?

Remember, a person's motivation is highly individualized, what do you team members each aspire to?

What part of their job do they find most enjoyable, or are they most proud of?

How does each team member like to be recognized and rewarded?

Day 17 – Organizational Learning

We've talked about the importance of being an adaptable leader, one who learns continuously. Your team has to be flexible and always learning, too.

Complacency is our worst enemy in a fast-changing environment, but we can combat it by continually re-evaluating the situation we're in, the people on our team, the tools we have, and the techniques we're using.

To fight complacency, leaders must also take time to reflect on everything we do personally. What went well, what did not, and what can we incrementally improve?

Feedback at this level can seem small, but it's not. Significant changes are always incremental and built on past experiences. The quick, natural feedback you get daily is what enables you to evolve to meet larger, more significant changes.

Your people may feel uncomfortable giving you feedback at first – as the leader; you have to ask for it. Don't just ask, require it. Doing so shows people that you view learning as more than what happens in quarterly or annual training.

Learning and development is work that no-one ever completes.

Think about the last project your team completed.

How would you describe the project?

What went well?
What needs to be improved on?

How do you team members answer these two questions?

Checkpoint 3:
Teach Your Team

Delegation is our #1 Teaching Tool.

Think a little bit further on some more of the tasks and processes that you can delegate to your team. Look at some of the tasks that you already delegate down, and see how you can continue to build your team member's experiences and roles though expanding on what you are currently passing down.

Reflect on a few small ways that you can incrementally grow and improve your team member's roles and responsibilities.

	Role	Responsibility	Next Step
1			
2			
3			
4			
5			

Now check your Next Steps using the questions in Days 13 and 14.

Day 18 – Leader's Roles—Planning

After sharing your relative vision, the next thing leaders have to do is plan how the team will get there. What course will you take toward the team's success, and how might you have to adapt those plans as events unfold.

Planning is tricky precisely because things change mid-stream. As a leader, it's your role to anticipate what changes are likely to come and think through how you'll deal with them ahead of time.

One of the best ways to do this is through scenario planning. Start by planning for two specific scenarios – the most likely outcome, and the most dangerous one. Make sure both are realistic in nature, not the doomsday, world-ending predictions that are highly unlikely and distracting. Pay special attention to small details. What has a high potential for de-railing specific steps along the way?

Think about an upcoming project for your team.

What are the critical steps?

What is the most likely scenario/outcome?

Remember to be as detail-orientated as possible, no-one climbs Mt. Everest in one day. What happens at each step along the way?

What is the most dangerous scenario/outcome. What are the greatest risks at each critical step?

Remember, this is not the world-ending scenario, this is the little slips that can have a large impact.
e.g. missed timelines, process failures, personnel changes, and other relatively likely events.

Day 19 – Leader's Roles—Equipping

Have you ever tried to cut your lawn with a pair of scissors? Probably not, because it would take forever. Having the right tools makes all the difference.

As a leader, we need to give our people the best tools we can reasonably provide to help them accomplish their mission. Before you set out, it's your job as a leader to make sure everything is in place, ready to use, and will be available when your people need it.

You have to make sure your team knows how to use those tools, too, and adapt them to different circumstances.

Sometimes, we have no choice but to work with what's available. That's when your experience and adaptability as a leader become a considerable asset. They are what enable you to think outside the box to find creative ways to use existing tools, supplies, and equipment that your people may not have come up with on their own.

Think a little more about your upcoming or current project.

What are the tools necessary to complete this project?

Computer software, hard tools, machine equipment, soft-skills and lines of communication ...

Who do we get them from?
Who maintains and updates them?

If something is missing or inadequate, what other sources may we find it or a replacement from?

Day 20 – Leader's Roles—Training

It doesn't do any good to have the best tools if no one knows how to use them. That's where training comes in.

Your training program should cover how to use key pieces of equipment, any company or industry standards and regulations the team must follow, and how to evaluate successful use of a resource.

Formal training, like employee on-boarding and classroom sessions, can cover a broad range of ideas, topics, and skills. It's best for training new people or showing current team members how to use new tools.

Informal training, such as peer-to-peer mentoring, should happen continuously. As a leader, you should encourage your team to share new ideas, best practices, and improvements with each other as they come up in the course of everyday work.

Think about your teams skills and goals.

What equipment, tools, and techniques are most important for my team right now?

What formal training do they receive on how to use and optimize the tools?

How can I foster informal training and mentoring across the team to share best-practices?

Day 21 – Leader's Roles—Supporting

Training prepares your people for the mission ahead, but as a leader we can't just train and go. You have to be there to support the team through tough times.

Supporting and facilitating our teams towards accomplishing their mission is our number one responsibility as leaders.

Our expertise, knowledge, and care go into everything that we do for our teams. Things will change, new ideas will be required, and problems will occur. There is nothing wrong with an "I don't know" so long as you then find the correct answer.

It is up to us to identify gaps and fill them before they become problems. Proactive support for our teams allows this to happen.

Think about your ongoing project.

How have my leaders supported me in the past?

In the future, my team will need the following kinds of support:

Materials — Knowledge — Emotional Support

I can provide this by:

Day 22 – Leader's Roles
—Providing Feedback

One specific type of support people need from their leader, one that's often undervalued, is feedback.

When you give feedback to team members, you help them take immediate action to correct what's not working and grow personally and professionally. Giving feedback to peers can build a stronger working relationship and better ties throughout the organization. Upward feedback allows managers and senior leaders to get a complete picture of the organization, including their impact on it, and make healthier, more well-informed decisions.

To be impactful feedback can't be given only quarterly or annually. It has to be continuous. Feedback isn't limited to standard reports or specific timelines like the performance review process. It is merely us talking to people about how they're doing and how we see what's happening in and around the team.

Most people have heard of the "feedback sandwich" – say something good, then a critique, and end with a second good thing. Great leaders don't necessarily use this formula. They don't try too hard to soften tough conversations. Instead, they keep things as positive as possible, while still being honest and constructive.

Great leaders also don't just complain about how bad things are. They pair constructive feedback with ideas and advice on how team members can improve.

It's important to remember that feedback isn't complicated. Even a simple *"thank you"* can be a powerful, effective way of telling your team they're doing a great job.

Growth and success is not possible without great feedback.

Some of my thoughts regarding my teams recent accomplishments are:

How did people perform? Did we meet or exceed our goals? How?

What needs to be fixed? How can they fix it?

Don't trap people in negative feedback. Provide constructive help towards their creation of a solution.

Who else in your organization needs to know something? What do they need to know?

How has their role affected your team? What do you need from them, more or less of what?

Checkpoint 4:
Your Role as a Leader

The five roles you play as a leader give you both the opportunity and responsibly to affect our team members, perform our tasks, and accomplish our missions a multitude of different ways. We all have varying comfort levels with each of these roles.

Think about your own comfort level, and reflect on how you can improve in each of them especially the areas where you are less comfortable.

Of the five roles I am most comfortable:

_____

_____

_____

I am least comfortable with:

_____

_____

_____

I can become more comfortable in these roles by:

_____

_____

_____

Next, ask a peer, coach, or mentor how they feel about your progress and development in each of these areas and what suggestions they would give you to improve.

Day 23 – Building Empathy

As leaders, we aren't really "in charge." The teams, missions, and people that we are responsible for are "in our charge."

Leadership isn't about power and authority; it's about stewardship - facilitating the success of other people while caring about and for them.

To fulfill this part of your leadership role, you need a healthy dose of empathy. You must have a keen sense of how your team is experiencing a situation and what they're feeling. That's hard, as each person will react to things differently.

Pay attention to specific signals that each team member gives when they're thinking or feeling a certain way. Being able to read non-verbal cues like this makes communication more effective – it can help you sense things that your team may not be ready or able to put into words.

Think about the current state of your team's morale.

The main things my team is going through right now are:

From what I've seen, I think they are feeling _____ about the current situation.

How might their feelings about the situation differ from mine given that I have different knowledge and life experience than they do?

Day 24 – Use of Authority

Caring for others is comfortable with our friends, but becomes much tougher when we throw deadlines and projects into the mix. We need to be able to draw the line and hold our teams accountable for their responsibilities.

The opposite side of our empathy is our ability to hold our teams accountable. We're here to accomplish a mission. We have a job to do, standards and deadlines to meet, and regulations to follow.

When a team member is struggling, think through what might be causing the problem. Is it something in the job itself, or an outside stressor in their lives? Is it a lack of training or equipment you have to fix to make them successful? Is it a poor fit or inadequate time to get the work done?

These are all things you control as a leader, but sometimes the problem is with the team member themselves. In that case, you may need to approach the situation with more authority than empathy – that good, old-fashioned tough love.

Tough love comes from both empathy and authority. It is up to us to care about not only what we accomplish, but the people that are working with us, and see that we handle everything in the best manner.

Think about a situation that is out of your direct control yet affects you.

What is the situation?
How is your team affected by it?

Will your team have to do something that they don't necessarily like, or aren't fully prepared for?

What metrics and benchmarks are in place to measure our progress and success?
How will we meet these?

Day 25 - Building Autonomy

Authority is about getting teams back on course if they go too far afield. Autonomy is about giving people the freedom to wander in the first place, to try things their way and make decisions independently.

As a leader, you have to give your team a sense of ownership over the tasks and roles assigned to them.

When personnel and teams are new to their roles they need more of your attention – feedback, progress checks, etc. – and perhaps less autonomy. However, as people get more competent at their job with time or training, don't be afraid to step back and let them do their job.

Giving others autonomy helps you, too. It lets you delegate more, focus on things only you can do, and foster collaboration within the group.

Think about your teams' progress in building their individual competencies.

Some new tasks and roles I think people can handle without me are:

I will check in to make sure they successful by:

How often and what am I looking for? Are measures and benchmarks appropriate and incremental?

Expanding their role to include more authority gives them and me benefits such as:

More time for me, better opportunities towards growth and promotion for them.

Day 26 – The Right Way to Use Oversight

As we said on Day 13, putting someone else in charge of a task doesn't absolve you – the leader – of responsibility. The buck still stops with you. You are ultimately responsible for making sure the work gets done well.

Oversight is how you balance the risk and responsibility.

The trick is finding the right level of oversight for the person and task at hand. Early on, you may be taking a risk with new team members or existing people taking on new roles. You're not sure if they can handle the work without supervision, so you practice more in-depth, more frequent oversight. As they gain experience and you gain confidence, you can scale the oversight back to a higher level.

Building autonomy slowly like this ensures that teams are ready to do the things we ask them to do the way they need to be done and gives them the confidence to take on even more autonomy as time goes by.

Providing the right level of oversight sooner, allows us to build more autonomy later.

Think about how you oversee you team's work.

I use the following to measure my team's progress and success:

What metrics and measurements do we use? Are we missing any?

These metrics are designed to incentivize:

What do these incentives actually drive our people to do? Is it in alignment with our vision, mission, and objectives?

How often do I check these benchmarks?

What trigger to change or act on any process exist? What are you looking for? What happens when things go well or go poorly?

Day 27 – Picking Metrics and Setting Goals

You can't manage what you don't measure. As a leader, you need a way to tell how close the team is to making your vision a reality and accomplishing the goals of their mission.

Above all else, the goals you set must be specific, easy-to-understand, and realistic. The metrics you use to track progress have to be transparent, too. Your team needs to know where the data is coming from and how you're using it to feel like they're being judged fairly.

Getting metrics and goals right is tricky, no matter the situation. Setting individual goals and tracking them in specific ways can incentivize behavior in ways you didn't intend. Leaders have to keep one eye on the purpose and one eye on how people are achieving those goals.

Look back at your team's goals from Day 16.

The status of our progress toward these goals is:

Do these goals aggregate and build on one another or are they separately measured?

Are our measurements genuinely objective, unbiased, fair, and grounded in what is possible?

Checkpoint 5:
Building your style

Building on the ideas from the last few days, it is important to note that the two pairs, empathy–authority and autonomy–oversight, exist on a continuum. How we act in each of these areas determines our leadership style.

There is no right answer for where on each continuum your leaders style should fall. However, all of us are more comfortable acting and managing our people in certain ways. Our challenge as leaders is that every person and situation calls for a different style and approach. Our approaches must be as diverse as the people we lead, and as expansive as the situations we find ourselves in.

Be knowledgeable about where your comfort zone is. But be ready to expand and act outside of it as your team's needs and situations change.

In the empathy–authority line I would place myself:

_____

_____

What situations call for me to act more on one end or the other? What would this look like?

_____

_____

On the autonomy–oversight line I am more comfortable interacting with my team by:

_____

_____

How can I move up and down the continuum as situations change?

_____

_____

Day 28 – Team Cohesion

We need to take the "team-building" out of building our teams.

Nothing brings people together like shared, mutually recognized success. As a leader, you need to understand individuals and connect their accomplishments to broader team wins. In acknowledging everyone's contributions to the whole, you help people see themselves as parts of a single, cohesive group.

Another way to build team cohesion is to use what you know about team members to create a sense of shared identity. What do your team members have in common outside of work? How can you help them help each other, encourage them to grow and develop together?

When someone devotes time to training or helping a co-worker, they get more invested in that co-worker's success. That type of caring is what ensures you will accomplish your mission together and build a collaborative culture within the team.

Think about you next team meeting.

What team milestones can you talk about and celebrate?

Who is going above and beyond in helping accomplish this milestone?

What are the best lessons each person can contribute from their past experience to make the team an even greater success?

Day 29 – Managing in 360°

Management is a two-way street, and you need to look both ways before crossing it.

As leaders, we have to do more than inform, support, and facilitate our teams. We must also take ownership of our role in the organization, managing upwards and across to our peers.

There's nothing worse than the feeling locked in a battle of 'us' versus 'them.' It's up to you to build the same sense of unity and cohesion across groups as you do within your own.

You also have to make sure communication flows clearly down to your people without things getting lost in translation. You don't like being handed work with only a vague sense of why you're doing it. Your people don't like it either, and they look to you to connect the dots.

Think about what information you're sending out and whom you're sending it to. None of us work in a bubble.

Think about what information you're sending out and who you're sending it to.

Who needs to understand my role, schedules, tasks, and team? What do they need to know?

Who do you interact with on a regular basis? Look higher, lower, and adjacent in your organization.

How have other people's decisions affected my team? Were they missing information when making those decisions?

How much visibility do others have into your world? How do they get this information?

How can you fill gaps and provide broader context and meaning to your traditional reports and metrics?

Day 30 – Putting it all together

Congratulations, you've reached the end of this guided tour of the first 30 days in your new leadership position. You have a better grasp of the tools and skills you need to succeed - now the real work starts.

To be a great leader, you can't just think about these things once. You have to build a set of beneficial, consistent habits around them.

I said at the start that knowledge is your most valuable asset as a leader. The notes you've made here are a record of what you know and what you've learned in your first month as a leader, so don't just put it on a shelf.

Use it as a reference - read and re-read it, especially when you get stuck or need inspiration.

The more you do, the stronger your knowledge will be of the fundamental concepts we've talked about here and the more adaptable and supportive a leader you'll be, and the more likely it is that your team will accomplish its mission.

As your last reflection exercise, look back on your entries from Day 1 and 2.

❖ How have you become more like your leadership role model?

❖ Were you successful in achieving your initial goals?

What are three things that you want to start, stop, and continue doing in the next 30, 90, and 365 days?

In the next 30 days I will:

In the next 90 days I will:

In the next year I will:

Conclusion: Embrace the Suck

We had a saying while the military that we used when someone was grumbling about the austere conditions in which we found ourselves. "Embrace the suck," we'd tell them.

Those words didn't change the situation. What they did was help us keep perspective and acknowledge that everyone was in the same boat. They broke the tension so we could laugh and continue about our business despite the conditions we faced.

Knowing you're part of a shared community helps you survive whatever hardships you find yourself in, and if you want to be a leader – especially an entrepreneur - there will be many.

Leadership is hard work. It is messy. It is late nights. It is continually putting out fires. It is the suck.

That's an important lesson to learn early in your journey. It is easy to look at someone's success story on Instagram, pictures of their "office view" from some poolside in Las Vegas, and think, "I can do that." What you don't see are all the trials and tribulations that person went through to get where they are or the 80 hours a week they put in to stay there.

It doesn't help that more and more these days, especially online, so-called experts are extolling the virtues and benefits of working for yourself while peddling a too-good-to-be-true 6-step program that "guarantees" success.

Real leaders don't gloss over the hard stuff. They may try to talk you out of becoming a leader or entrepreneur by giving you the good, the bad, and the ugly to see if you're up for the challenge.

I saw this recently during a Veterans Entrepreneurial training class I co-hosted with the Small Business Administration (SBA) and Endicott College. We had 16 veterans who had recently separated from the military show up for a crash course in being your own boss. By lunch, more than half had left.

From the start, the experience felt like drinking from a firehose, and once they'd seen how much knowledge, hard work, blood, sweat, and tears go into creating a successful venture, they decided it's not for them. At first, my co-hosts and I were disappointed by the exodus, but in reality, it was both necessary and a good thing.

Successful leaders and entrepreneurs have to embrace the suck. You have to prepare for the long, arduous hours and move past the glamorous facade the media portrays. Once you become successful, you also need to do your part to stop glamorizing successes and better inform people about the realities they will face in this field.

This community has – and should share – its incredible success stories. I see them around me every day. Just don't pat yourself on the back for too long. Richelieu Dennis, CEO of Sundial Brands, said what all good leaders say in his acceptance speech after being inducted into The Babson College Entrepreneurial Hall of Fame, "It is time for me to get back to work."

Only through hard work, persistent effort, continued growth, and learning will you become a success story. You've jump-started the journey with this journal. Now it's time to get to work - embrace your own suck.

If you liked this book, continue your daily learning at https://lrn.st/learnmore

About Arist:

Arist is recognized in Fast Company's 2019 List of World Changing Ideas. Arist started with a simple realization: access to digital education is extremely unequal. Concerned by the lack of educational resources in war-torn Yemen, Arist's founders began exploring ways to teach entrepreneurship to teens in a conflict zone halfway around the world. They found that only 30% of students in Yemen had consistent access to the internet, but nearly every student, had access to text messages.

About the Author:

Ed Brzychcy is the founder of Blue Cord Management, LLC, a Boston based Leadership Development Consultancy. This book is developed from Blue Cord Management's 'Lead from the Front' training program.

Ed uses strategies and techniques inspired by his military experience throughout Blue Cord Management's programming. He served with distinction for twelve years from 1999 to 2011 as an intelligence analyst and infantryman, achieving the rank of Staff Sergeant, and leading squads of up to a dozen soldiers during three combat deployments to Iraq.

Ed earned his Bachelor's Degree from Salem State University and was later awarded an MBA from Babson College. He holds an Adjunct Professor position at Endicott College in Beverly, MA where he teaches classes in Business Fundamentals, Leadership, and Entrepreneurship.

Last Words and Special Offer

If you're like me, you may hesitate to mark up or write on your book.

Because of that we have created a companion workbook containing each day's exercises and checkpoints.

Goto https://leadership.bluecordmgmt.com/ NewLeaderWorkbook and enter code: NEWLEADER to receive a discounted copy of the workbook.

Good luck on your leadership journey.

Ed Brzychcy

Made in the USA
Columbia, SC
24 July 2019